The Military History of World War II
Volume 6

THE AIR WAR IN THE WEST
September 1939 — May 1941

The Military History of World War II: Volume 6

THE AIR WAR
IN THE WEST
September 1939 – May 1941

by Trevor Nevitt Dupuy
COL., U.S. ARMY, RET.

FRANKLIN WATTS, INC.
575 Lexington Avenue • New York 22

TO TINA

Contents

The Military History of World War II
Volume 6

THE AIR WAR IN THE WEST
September 1939 — May 1941

A tight formation of Junkers JU-57 dive bombers. They are about to spread out to attack individual targets.

The *Luftwaffe* and *Blitzkrieg*

Hitler and German Rearmament

ON JANUARY 30, 1933, President Paul von Hindenburg appointed Adolf Hitler chancellor of Germany. Less than fifteen years earlier, in World War I, Hindenburg had commanded the German army, and Hitler had been an obscure corporal in that army. World War I had been ended by the Treaty of Versailles, in which the victorious Allies had made Germany pay for damages its army had inflicted on Allied countries during the war. It had also forced Germany to give up parts of its territory to France, Poland, and Denmark. The treaty had permitted Germany to have only a small army and a small navy. It had forbidden that defeated country to have an air force.

In the years following the war, Germany had been torn by serious political and economic disturbances. The German people, feeling that their democratic government offered them little hope for the future, had grown bitter and discouraged. Hitler had been able to persuade many of them to join and support his National Socialist, or Nazi party by telling them that Germany would be rich again if they would just tear up the Treaty of Versailles and refuse to accept its terms. He had said that none of the former Allies would dare interfere; Germany could take its rightful "place in the sun" as the most powerful country in Europe.

Many of the German people had been anxious to revive their country's old-time glories, and Hitler was a stirring and persuasive orator. He had become so popular that his former commanding officer was forced to make him chancellor.

In a few months Hitler took over complete governmental power and made himself dictator of Germany. Immediately he began secret

1

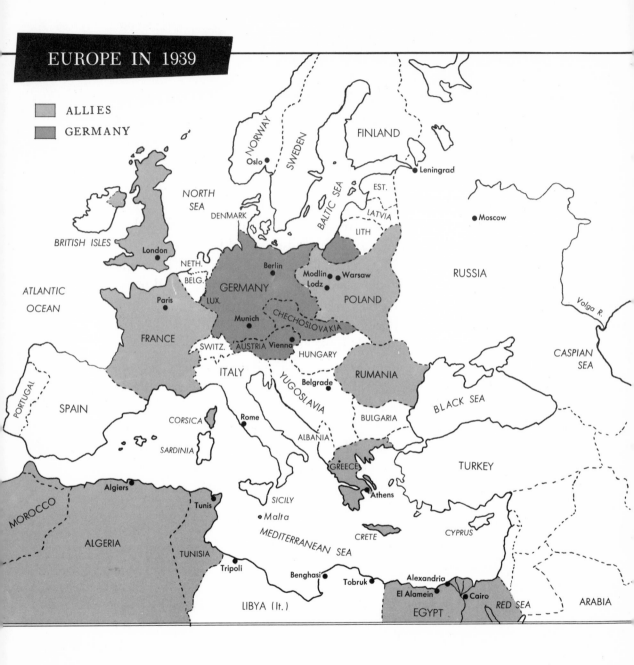

EUROPE IN 1939

ALLIES
GERMANY

NORWAY
SWEDEN
FINLAND
Oslo
Leningrad
NORTH
SEA
EST.
DENMARK
LATVIA
BALTIC SEA
LITH.
Moscow
BRITISH ISLES
London
NETH.
Berlin
Modlin Warsaw
RUSSIA
BELG.
GERMANY
Lodz
POLAND
ATLANTIC
OCEAN
Paris
LUX.
Munich
CHECHOSLOVAKIA
Volga R.
FRANCE
SWITZ. AUSTRIA Vienna
HUNGARY
CASPIAN
SEA
PORTUGAL
ITALY
RUMANIA
SPAIN
Belgrade
CORSICA
Rome
YUGOSLAVIA
BLACK SEA
BULGARIA
SARDINIA
ALBANIA
TURKEY
GREECE
Algiers
SICILY
Athens
MOROCCO
Tunis
Malta
CYPRUS
ALGERIA
MEDITERRANEAN SEA
CRETE
TUNISIA
Tripoli
Benghasi
Tobruk
Alexandria
ARABIA
LIBYA (It.)
El Alamein
Cairo
RED SEA
EGYPT

preparations to strengthen the German army and navy and to create a new *Luftwaffe*, or air force. But while he did this, he assured the rest of the world that he was really a peaceful man who had no intention of violating the Treaty of Versailles. The rest of the world so desperately wanted peace that it was ready to believe him.

A Lonely Warning

ONE MAN, however, did not believe Hitler. This was an English politician and writer named Winston Churchill. As a young man, during World War I, Churchill had had a distinguished career in the British government. Now none of the three largest political parties in England wanted him. They did not like his persistent habit of pointing out unpleasant, unpopular truths.

Churchill had studied the lessons of World War I. He had also studied Hitler's writings and speeches. He knew that new factories for weapons and airplanes were being built in Germany, and that a country as highly industrialized as Germany could build a large air force in a very few years. This would be the quickest and most effective way for that country to build up its military strength. He was sure that Hitler fully intended to make Germany a great military power — if the rest of the world would let him do it.

As early as 1933, Churchill had made speeches in the English House of Commons warning his countrymen of this danger. As time went on, he saw his predictions fulfilled. Hitler's rearmament program was now so vast that he could not keep it entirely hidden. Churchill told the House of Commons that the German air force was already as large as Britain's, and that if England did not immediately start building airplanes, the *Luftwaffe* would be twice as strong as the Royal Air Force by 1937.

All this Mr. Stanley Baldwin, the British Prime Minister, denied. He insisted that British air strength was much greater than Germany's, and would remain so. Since people were sure that the Prime Minister must know what he was talking about, nobody paid any more attention to what Churchill said.

Churchill repeated his warnings in 1934. This time Mr. Baldwin had to confess that Churchill was right, and that he himself had been terribly wrong. He admitted that the German *Luftwaffe* was already at least as large as Britain's Royal Air Force. He then added that, recognizing his error of the year before, he and his government were taking immediate steps to increase the size of the Royal Air Force. This satisfied most people. They applauded Baldwin's manful admission of error and expressed admiration of his determination to build up Britain's air strength.

But Churchill knew, just as well as Hitler and the officers of the British and German air forces knew, that it is not possible to start a large aircraft construction program overnight. Germany had been preparing for such a program even before Hitler came into power. And now it had a two-year head start in the aircraft production race.

Just as Baldwin had promised, the British started to expand their aircraft production. But the Germans kept increasing their lead. Churchill continued his warnings, insisting that British efforts were not intensive enough, but most Englishmen remained deaf to his predictions of coming disaster.

The Tragedy of Munich

By 1938, Hitler was satisfied that German air strength was far greater than the combined strengths of Britain and France. Those two countries would surely be afraid to risk a war. The time had

Adolf Hitler, with Field Marshal Goering beside him, stands on the balcony of the Reich Chancellery to acknowledge the cheers of the crowd.

U.S. ARMY PHOTOGRAPH

come for Germany to begin its program of expansion by gobbling up small neighboring nations.

In March, 1938, Hitler tested his theories by seizing Austria. Just as he had expected, nobody did anything about it. In September he threatened Czechoslovakia, which was allied to Britain and France. The Czechs prepared to fight, and called on France and England to help them.

By this time the British government knew just how far behind the *Luftwaffe* the Royal Air Force had fallen. Prime Minister Neville Chamberlain had followed the same policies as his predecessor, Mr. Baldwin, and he reacted to Czechoslovakia's plea for help just as Hitler had guessed he would. He was afraid to stand by his small ally if that meant involving Britain in a war with Germany. And so, in a disgraceful political deal at Munich, Chamberlain and Prime Minister Edouard Daladier of France agreed to Hitler's taking over a small part of Czechoslovakia. Hitler said that this was all he wanted and promised that Germany would not need any more territory. Five

5

COMBAT AIR STRENGTHS, SUMMER 1939

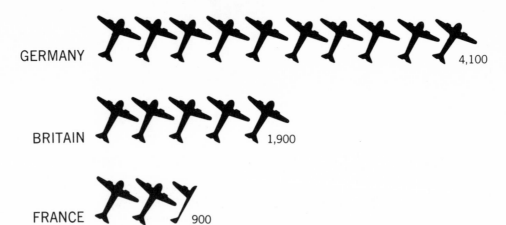

GERMANY 4,100

BRITAIN 1,900

FRANCE 900

POLAND 500

months later he broke that promise and occupied all of Czechoslovakia. Britain and France made no move to stop him.

The surrender at Munich and Hitler's seizure of the whole of Czechoslovakia made the British people realize at last that Churchill had been right all along. Now England did start a tremendous airplane construction program. The British knew they were so far behind Hitler that they had no hope of catching up, but at least they were determined not to fall back any farther. And they had reason to hope that their newer and better planes and other modern equipment would make up somewhat for what their air force lacked in size.

By the summer of 1939, the Royal Air Force had 100,000 men and over 1,900 combat-ready planes. But the *Luftwaffe* had a strength of 500,000 men, with more than 4,100 combat-ready aircraft. France, England's strongest ally, had less than 1,000 planes.

The Invasion of Poland

IN AUGUST, 1939, Hitler tried to gobble up Poland just as he had gobbled up Czechoslovakia. This time Mr. Chamberlain and Mr. Daladier knew they could not back down. When Hitler invaded Poland on September 1, 1939, France and England declared war against Germany. They soon realized, however, that there was little they could do to help the brave but unprepared Poles.

At dawn on September 1, 1939, German air fleets totaling more than sixteen hundred planes began to sweep over Poland. Reichsmarshal Hermann Goering, commander in chief of the *Luftwaffe,* was in direct control of the air operations. Goering was a fat, pompous man who liked to wear fancy uniforms decorated with rows of medals. He had been a fighter pilot in World War I, and after the war had become one of the first members of Hitler's Nazi party. Now Goering was the second most powerful man in Germany. Although he was not a very good military commander, he was a very shrewd politician. He also knew a good military commander when he saw one. In direct command of his air fleets attacking Poland he had put two superb air officers: General Albert Kesselring and General Hugo Sperrle.

The Poles had about five hundred combat aircraft, most of them modern. The Polish pilots were skillful and courageous, but they had very little chance to show their skill; the German attacks caught them completely by surprise. By noon of the first day of the war, most of the Polish planes had been destroyed on their airfields before they even had a chance to get into the air. Wave after wave of German Stuka dive bombers hit the Polish airfields. The bombers were followed by fast Messerschmitt 109 fighter planes that sprayed the hangars and barracks with machine-gun fire. The few Polish planes that managed to get into the air were quickly shot down by the

7

Junkers JU-52 bomber plane.

Germans. By September 3, the Polish air force had been destroyed.

Having won complete control of the air, the *Luftwaffe* was now able to devote all of its efforts to helping the German ground armies that had already begun to smash their way through Polish defenses. To prevent the Poles from moving their mobilized reserves to the front, the German planes first concentrated their attacks against roads and railroads. German bombers struck the railroad switching and marshaling yards in Polish cities and knocked out railroad and road bridges. At the same time, German fighter planes swept along the railroad tracks, shooting at moving trains; they swarmed over Polish roads to attack columns of trucks and marching soldiers.

Spies sent back information about the location of the headquarters of the Polish army, so German planes were able to bomb it and prevent it from properly controlling the fighting ground troops. Marshal Edward Smigly-Rydz, the Polish commander, moved army headquarters repeatedly but, helped by the spies, the German planes found it every time. The Polish armies had to fight without any effective overall command.

Meantime, large German high-level bombers had begun to attack Polish war industries in order to halt Polish manufacture of weapons, airplanes, and equipment. Night and day, bombs exploded in the industrial sections of all the Polish cities.

By September 12, all communications and industry in Poland were paralyzed, but the Polish army was still fighting bravely against the German ground invaders. Polish troops had repulsed a hasty German assault on Warsaw and were actually trying to counterattack near Lodz. Some German dive bombers and fighter planes had been giving assistance to German ground troops; now, with the Polish air force totally destroyed, Goering shifted most of his remaining air fleets to join in the support of the *Wehrmacht* — the German army.

Since the *Luftwaffe* had destroyed the bridges and railroads, the Polish armies west of Warsaw could not retreat. They were ham-

German bombers strike the suburbs of Warsaw.

mered mercilessly by Stuka dive bombers, and by Dornier and Heinkel high-level bombers. They were subjected to endless machine-gun strafings by the Messerschmitt fighters, slashed by hard-hitting tank columns, and assaulted by tough German infantry soldiers. The magnificent courage of the Polish army could not stand up against the cold and ruthless efficiency of these overwhelming air and ground attacks. By September 17, more than 250,000 Polish soldiers had surrendered in western Poland. But isolated groups continued to fight valiantly around Warsaw and elsewhere in the country.

As the German ground forces continued their inexorable advance eastward, the German air force shifted its attacks to strike these isolated concentrations of Polish troops. It was only a matter of time. One by one these grimly determined defenders were subjected to the same sort of hammering that had destroyed the central Polish armies. Warsaw and Modlin surrendered on September 27, with 130,000 men. The last remnant of the Polish army surrendered on October 5.

Blitzkrieg *and Air Power*

THE WORLD had been given its first view of a new method of warfare which the Germans called *blitzkrieg* — lightning war. But really this *blitzkrieg* — with one exception — was simply an up-to-date, motorized and mechanized version of efficient ground warfare as it had always been fought by well-trained soldiers and intelligent generals. It was simply that tanks had been substituted for horse cavalry, and trucks and tractors were replacing horse-drawn wagons.

One vital element of *blitzkrieg*, however, was completely new. This was the massive use of air power, which had paralyzed the railroads and communications of Poland, which had terrified the civilian popu-

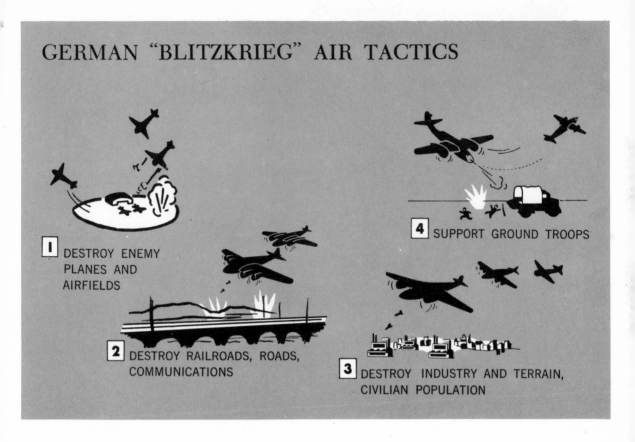

GERMAN "BLITZKRIEG" AIR TACTICS

1 DESTROY ENEMY PLANES AND AIRFIELDS

2 DESTROY RAILROADS, ROADS, COMMUNICATIONS

3 DESTROY INDUSTRY AND TERRAIN, CIVILIAN POPULATION

4 SUPPORT GROUND TROOPS

lation, and which had supported the German ground armies with pulverizing aerial assaults of a kind never seen before.

In one month of fighting the *Luftwaffe* had given the world a terrifying demonstration of the potentialities of air power. A new dimension, and new frightfulness, had been added to war.

11

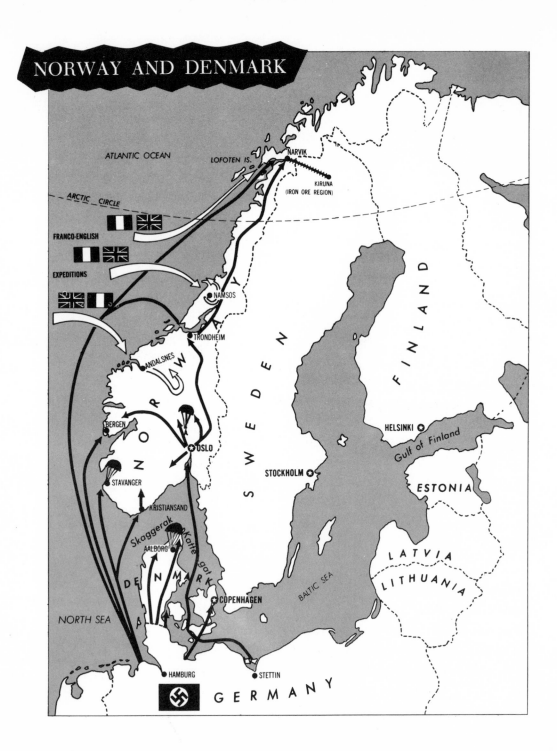

NORWAY AND DENMARK

ATLANTIC OCEAN

LOFOTEN IS.

NARVIK

KIRUNA
(IRON ORE REGION)

ARCTIC CIRCLE

FRANCO-ENGLISH

EXPEDITIONS

NAMSOS

FINLAND

TRONDHEIM

N O R W A Y

ANDALSNES

S W E D E N

BERGEN

HELSINKI

Gulf of Finland

STAVANGER

OSLO

STOCKHOLM

ESTONIA

KRISTIANSAND

Skaggerak

Katte gat

AALBORG

D E N M A R K

LATVIA

LITHUANIA

COPENHAGEN

BALTIC SEA

NORTH SEA

HAMBURG

STETTIN

G E R M A N Y

Terror in the West

The "Phony War"

WHILE POLAND was dying in agony, Britain and France did little to help their stricken ally. Neither country had bombers of long enough range to reach the Polish battlefields, but France had a powerful army that could have attacked the weak garrisons defending western Germany. Such attacks would have forced Hitler to pull back troops from Poland and would have reduced pressure on the Polish armies. And if British and French planes had attacked targets in Germany, Goering would probably have been forced to withdraw some of his air units from Poland to meet the Allied threat.

British bomber planes did fly over Germany — but only to drop propaganda leaflets. French soldiers sat in their trenches — and so did the British troops when they arrived in France in September and October of 1939. And so some people called this the *sitzkrieg.* Others called it the "phony war." During the winter of 1939-1940, the only real military activity was a few small air raids by both sides against naval bases and airfields.

In Germany, however, the time was not being wasted. The *Wehrmacht* and the *Luftwaffe* were getting ready to make more use of their new *blitzkrieg.* And Hitler was planning to use psychological warfare as well.

German photographers had taken excellent motion pictures of the *blitzkrieg* in Poland. These were put together in a propaganda film which particularly emphasized the terrible destruction which the *Luftwaffe* had spread across Poland. The Germans showed these pictures in many of the small neutral countries of Europe. The terrified people of these countries understood very well what Hitler meant. They knew that they had better cooperate with Germany, or they would suffer the same kind of destruction. In Norway, in particular, the German ambassador made sure that the pictures were seen by all the leading citizens.

The Invasion of Norway

DURING THE WINTER of 1939–1940, Hitler decided that he must conquer Norway. Germany's war industry depended upon iron ore from Sweden, which was shipped to Germany by way of Narvik in Norway. Hitler wanted to make sure that he controlled this important supply route. He also knew that if Germany was in possession of the long coast of Norway, the British would have great difficulty in continuing their naval blockade of Germany. Finally, the German dictator wanted to establish air bases in Norway from which to attack northern England and Scotland.

A Royal Air Force Lockheed Hudson reconnaissance bomber scores a hit on a German supply ship from a height of 8,000 feet in the harbor of Tyboron, Denmark.

On April 9, 1940, Hitler launched his attack against Norway by invading Denmark. He wanted Denmark for a sort of stepping-stone to Norway. Possession of Denmark would also give Germany control over vital sea routes in the Baltic Sea. Early that April morning German troops swarmed over the little country and conquered it in twelve hours, almost without a fight. At the same time, the *Luftwaffe* streaked out of the sky to destroy the Norwegian air force on the ground, just as it had destroyed the Polish air force. German soldiers, arriving secretly by sea, thronged ashore at the Norwegian ports of Narvik, Trondheim, Bergen, and Kristiansand. The German navy tried to escort troop transports to Oslo, but was repulsed by Norwegian coast defense troops. Here were some Norwegians who had seen Hitler's propaganda movies, and had not been frightened by them.

The courageous defense of Oslo Fjord failed to stop the Germans. Transport planes dropped paratroops, who quickly captured Oslo's airfield. More paratroops seized the airfield at Stavanger. Then a force of five hundred German transport planes began to ferry more troops and equipment to the captured airfields. The tiny Norwegian army continued to fight, but it was outnumbered. Supported by *Luftwaffe* planes, German troop columns raced over the roads of Norway, overrunning most of the country.

Britain and France attempted to land troops near Trondheim and near Narvik. Royal Air Force fighter planes, sent to Norway in aircraft carriers, started to set up a base on a frozen lake near Trondheim. Goering immediately rushed German air reinforcements to Norway under the command of *Luftwaffe* General Erhard Milch. And at the same time German ground troops continued to pour in by plane. Before the Allies could get themselves established near Trondheim, they were struck by overwhelming air and ground attacks and forced to withdraw. Only one Royal Air Force plane got away.

15

Meanwhile, German planes had begun to attack the British navy ships that supported Allied operations close to the Norwegian shore. This was the first battle in history between air and naval forces. The *Luftwaffe* won. They inflicted so much damage that the British ships had to pull away from the coast. This made it easier for the German ground troops to complete the occupation of southern and central Norway.

At Narvik, however, the Germans ran into trouble. The town was so far north that they could not mount as intensive air attacks against the British navy as they had off southern Norway. At Narvik the British had flown some fighter planes ashore from carriers, and a seesaw fight on land and in the air continued for nearly a month. Finally the British captured the town, but soon after, momentous events elsewhere forced them to withdraw. By June 9, the German conquest of Norway was complete.

This Gloster Gladiator, grounded for lack of fuel, was the only plane that remained of eighteen that flew into central Norway to provide fighter protection to British troops trying to drive back the invading Germans.

The Invasion of France and the Low Countries

DURING THE CONQUEST OF NORWAY, Hitler and his military staffs had been making plans for a much greater military operation. This was to be a gigantic invasion of Holland, Belgium, and France. Hitler's victories in Poland, Denmark, and Norway had made him confident that his armies and air fleets could defeat the combined military strengths of England and France, plus the smaller forces of Holland and Belgium.

Ten armies, totaling more than 2,000,000 men, were to take part in the invasion. To support them, the *Luftwaffe* had assembled 3,900 combat planes — three-quarters of its total strength. The planes included more than 1,100 long-range bombers, nearly 400 dive bombers, and about 1,300 fighter planes. The remainder were reconnaissance and other special-purpose aircraft. To oppose this great air armada, there were only about 700 French planes and 400 British planes based in France.

As in the Polish campaign, Goering was in overall command of the *Luftwaffe* forces for the invasion of the West. As in Poland, most of the actual direction and control of the air operations was done by the commanders of the two air fleets — General Kesselring for Air Fleet Two, and General Hans-Juergen Stumpff for Air Fleet Three. Their principal mission was to assist the *Wehrmacht* ground attack, and so they coordinated their plans directly with the senior ground commanders.

The great invasion was heralded on May 10, 1940, by a series of violent, predawn *Luftwaffe* attacks against Holland and Belgium. There was no warning; there was no declaration of war. The neutral Dutch and Belgians knew they were at war only when their countries were shattered by explosions, flames, and flying slivers of steel.

17

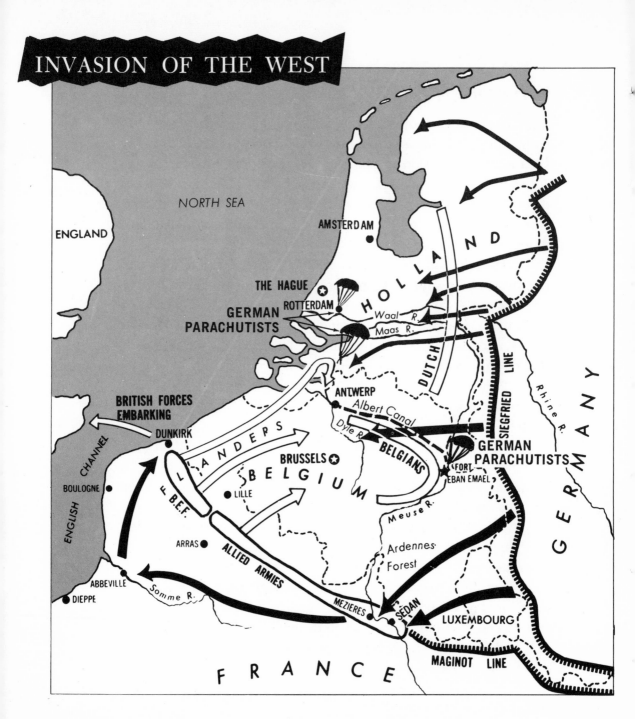

INVASION OF THE WEST

NORTH SEA

ENGLAND

AMSTERDAM

HOLLAND

THE HAGUE
ROTTERDAM
GERMAN
PARACHUTISTS

Waal R.
Maas R.

DUTCH LINE

SIEGFRIED LINE

Rhine R.

GERMANY

BRITISH FORCES
EMBARKING

DUNKIRK

ANTWERP
Albert Canal

Dyle R.
BELGIANS

GERMAN
PARACHUTISTS

FLANDERS

B.E.F.

BOULOGNE

ENGLISH CHANNEL

BRUSSELS

BELGIUM

LILLE

FORT
EBAN EMAEL

Meuse R.

ARRAS

ALLIED ARMIES

Ardennes
Forest

ABBEVILLE

DIEPPE

Somme R.

MEZIERES

SEDAN

LUXEMBOURG

MAGINOT LINE

FRANCE

Airfields were the main targets, and most of the small air forces of the two little countries were smashed on the ground. But German planes also struck ground military installations, headquarters, and communications centers. Holland was hit particularly hard.

Then, at dawn, while German tanks and infantrymen swept across the borders of Holland and Belgium, waves of German transport planes, loaded with paratroopers, flew overhead. Some of these planes discharged their cargoes of airborne soldiers over the airfields near The Hague, the Dutch capital. Other paratroopers were dropped near the main bridges over the Maas, Waal, and Lek rivers — the estuaries of the Meuse and Rhine rivers just before they empty into the North Sea. Control of these bridges was vital to the Germans if their tanks were to sweep through to the heart of Holland.

One more group of paratroops landed on top of Fort Eben Emael, the key of the Belgian defense line in northeastern Belgium. This underground fortress had been built to defy the heaviest possible ground attack — but it was defenseless against airborne troops, who quickly got inside it through ventilators and trapdoors on the top.

Dutch counterattacks drove the German paratroopers from the

Rotterdam's airport, following a raid by Hitler's Luftwaffe.

German planes carrying supplies to the German army in Belgium.

airfields near The Hague. But this used up all of the Dutch reserves, who would otherwise have been able to help their battered frontline comrades. The other German airborne units held their objectives, and soon German tank columns were dashing across the Maas and the Waal river bridges into the very center of Holland.

Rotterdam

WELL INTO the little country now, the Germans were suddenly held up by fierce Dutch resistance near Rotterdam. On May 14, upon the personal orders of Hitler, the German ground commander demanded the surrender of Rotterdam, warning the Dutch commander that if the city was not given up immediately, it would be bombed by the *Luftwaffe*. Goering had apparently suggested this to Hitler. He had been waiting for an opportunity to terrorize the civilian populations of the Western democracies. Without waiting for the Dutch to reply to Hitler's ultimatum, Goering ordered his bombers to Rotterdam. While the local Dutch commander was still negotiating for the surrender of the city, several waves of German bombers struck the center of the city. In a short while the heart of Rotterdam was completely destroyed. Nearly a thousand people were killed, several thousand were wounded, and almost eighty thousand were homeless.

This terrible, ruthless act had the effect Hitler and Goering wanted; Rotterdam capitulated immediately. The Dutch government fled Holland to seek refuge in England. The Dutch army surrendered to the Germans the next day. While part of the German armies in the north continued the occupation of Holland, the remainder swept southward to join the other forces already deep inside Belgium.

The Fall of France

The Battle for Flanders

THE FIRST GERMAN AIR ATTACKS on May 10 had reached the airfields of northern France, but the French and British squadrons had received sufficient warning so that very few planes were lost on the ground. The air battle for supremacy over Belgium and northern France began immediately, while French and British ground troops rushed northward into Belgium to help their new allies.

In England, people had become increasingly dissatisfied with Prime Minister Chamberlain. When news of the German invasion reached London, Chamberlain was forced to resign. He was replaced by Winston Churchill, whose early, prophetic warnings had now been proven right. Taking control immediately, he sent two Royal Air Force fighter squadrons to France to reinforce the ten already there.

During the first four days of bitter air fighting over Belgium and northern France, losses were heavy on both sides. The Royal Air

Flying Officer Edgar J. Kain, of the Royal Air Force, first British pilot to receive the Distinguished Flying Cross awarded pilots serving in France.

A camouflage net conceals a British plane somewhere in France.

Force found that their planes and pilots had a slight edge over those of the Germans. The British were particularly pleased with the performance of their Hurricane fighter planes. Although the Messerschmitt 109 was theoretically a slightly superior aircraft, particularly at high altitudes, the maneuverable Hurricanes, with their eight machine guns, were more than holding their own over the battle lines. And the British had an even newer and better plane — the Spitfire — which had not yet been in action.

The French were not doing so well. They had some good planes, and they had some good pilots. But they also had many very poor pilots, and the entire air force was poorly organized. After four or five days of fighting, the French air force was close to collapsing.

At this time — May 14 — the German ground troops sprang the trap they had been preparing for the Allies. While British and French troops had been moving into central Belgium, the main German

German officers examine a burned plane at Le Bourget airport in France.

armies had been advancing around their right flank, through the mountainous Forest of Ardennes, in eastern Belgium.

The Belgians and the French had thought that the poor roads of the rugged Ardennes would prevent the Germans from trying a large-scale movement in that region. They were completely surprised when hordes of German troops and tanks reached the Meuse River at Sedan and Mézières, in France. Rushing across the river, the Germans soon made a fifty-mile hole in the thin Allied lines. German tank columns raced through the gap. They were now behind the main British and French field armies.

24

All of the available Royal Air Force planes in France were concentrated against this threat. Their principal objective was to destroy the ponton bridges which the Germans had built over the Meuse River. As the British planes made their attacks, German fighters rushed to meet them. German antiaircraft guns sent up barrages around the vital bridges. Despite heroic efforts, the British were unable to destroy the bridges. And although they shot down fifty-three German planes, they lost nearly seventy themselves. Realizing that they could not continue to take such losses, the British had to give up their attacks on the Meuse bridges, and devote their remaining strength to the support of their hard-pressed ground army.

With their own air force now almost completely destroyed, the French begged for more British air units to be sent from England. Churchill sent them some, dangerously weakening the strength of the Royal Air Force's Fighter Command, which was responsible for the air defense of Britain. When the French asked him for still more planes, he had to refuse them. Whatever happened in France, Churchill knew that England's survival depended upon its security from air attack.

A German Messerschmitt brought down by French antiaircraft guns.

Dunkirk

MEANWHILE, the Allied ground forces in Belgium and northern France had been completely cut off by the main German drive across the Meuse. That drive had now reached the English Channel near Abbeville. With the Germans pressing in on them from three sides, British, French, and Belgian troops fell back to the North Sea coast of French and Belgian Flanders. Then the Belgians surrendered. There was nothing left for the British and French to do but to try to escape to Britain by sea.

Churchill knew that now he would have to put more planes into the fight. He must not only prevent the *Luftwaffe* from smashing the British army on the beaches, but also give some protection to the navy and civilian ships rushing from Britain to rescue the defeated armies on the beaches near Dunkirk.

British soldiers aim their rifles at German aircraft during the evacuation of Dunkirk.

A Royal Air Force Lockheed Hudson flies toward Dunkirk on a reconnaissance patrol.

Single-seat British Spitfire fighting planes.

*German Heinkel HE-
111 bomber rises from
an airfield in France.*

Goering, meanwhile, had asked Hitler to give the *Luftwaffe* a chance to have a full share in the glory of the great German victory. Goering had assured Hitler that his planes could completely destroy the British and French ground troops. None would escape. Hitler had approved Goering's idea and told his generals to stop the German ground advance.

As the *Luftwaffe* pilots closed in for the kill, however, they suddenly found themselves engaged in a full-scale air battle with the reinforced Royal Air Force. And this time there were Spitfires as well as Hurricanes in the battle. From May 28 to June 2 the vicious air conflict raged over Dunkirk and nearby areas of the North Sea and of Flanders. And while it went on, ships and small boats ferried the surviving soldiers from Dunkirk back to England. These boats evacuated 225,000 British troops, and 113,000 French and Belgian troops. The British people called this the "Miracle of Dunkirk." In a way it *was* a miracle, but it was accomplished only because of the courage and skill of the sailors who took the troops away, and the courage and skill of the Royal Air Force fighter pilots who kept the German planes so busy that they were unable to interfere seriously.

29

Oil tanks at Le Havre, France, set afire by Luftwaffe *planes.*

The Battle of France

ON JUNE 5 the Germans resumed their ground attacks into central France. As usual, the *Wehrmacht* was supported by intensive air attacks. The *Luftwaffe* destroyed airfields, army headquarters, road and railroad bridges, and attacked moving columns on the roads. Since the roads were clogged with refugees trying to escape from the war zone, many civilians were killed. This added to the terror of the refugees, and clogged the roads still more.

Churchill had sent as many Royal Air Force planes as possible to help the French, since France now had no effective air force of its own. He did this despite the strong protests of Air Chief Marshal Hugh C. T. Dowding, commander in chief of the Royal Air Force's Fighter Command, who was responsible for the air defense of Britain. Dowding was left with less than five hundred aircraft, although he thought he needed at least nine hundred. But Churchill felt that England would have to take this risk, in order to do everything possible to save her ally.

It was not possible to save France, however. The French armies collapsed. On June 17, aged Marshal Henri Pétain, a hero of World War I, became the new prime minister of a defeated France. He immediately asked Hitler for an armistice. On June 25, as the surviving British planes flew back to England, France surrendered to Germany.

From the beginning of the German attacks on May 10 until the French surrender, the British lost 959 planes. Of these, 477 were fighters; the remainder were bombers, reconnaissance planes and transports. This was about 40 per cent of the total active strength of the Royal Air Force. Losses such as these were staggering. Though the Germans had lost about as many planes, these represented only about 20 per cent of the total strength of the *Luftwaffe*. And in addition, the Germans had knocked out the entire French air force.

At the end of June, 1940, the situation looked dismal for the British.

A British bomber shot down somewhere in occupied France.

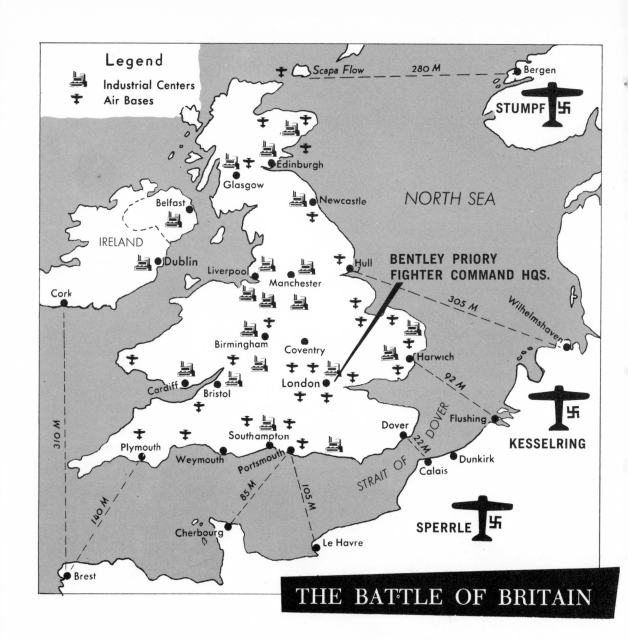

Legend

Industrial Centers

Air Bases

Scapa Flow   280 M   Bergen

STUMPF

Edinburgh

Glasgow

Newcastle   NORTH SEA

Belfast

IRELAND

Dublin

Liverpool   Hull   BENTLEY PRIORY
                                     FIGHTER COMMAND HQS.

Cork   Manchester
                                                    305 M   Wilhelmshaven

Birmingham   Coventry
                                        Harwich
Cardiff   Bristol   London   92 M
                                                    Flushing
                                        Dover
                                                    KESSELRING
             Southampton   22 M   STRAIT OF DOVER
Plymouth   Calais   Dunkirk
         Weymouth   Portsmouth
310 M   85 M   105 M

                                        SPERRLE
140 M   Cherbourg

                         Le Havre
Brest

THE BATTLE OF BRITAIN

The Battle of Britain—Preliminaries

Operation SEA LION

AFTER DUNKIRK, Hitler briefly considered an immediate airborne invasion of Britain before completing the conquest of France. This was recommended by Colonel General Erhard Milch, now inspector general of the *Luftwaffe*. But Goering disapproved the idea, and other German military men were dubious.

The British army had lost most of its guns, tanks, and other heavy equipment, but both the Royal Air Force and the Royal Navy were still intact, even though badly battered. Most German military men believed that they must have absolute control of the air before an airborne invasion could be successful. And many doubted that even with unchallenged air superiority the *Luftwaffe* could fly in enough reinforcements and supplies to the airborne troops. The build-up would have to go by sea. The German navy could not challenge British control of the surface of the sea; the *Luftwaffe* would have to do this, as they had near Norway. But the German air fleets would not be able to drive the British navy from the Strait of Dover until they had obtained air superiority over the coast of Britain.

The German military staffs believed, therefore, that for either an airborne or water-borne invasion of England, the first step must be to drive the Royal Air Force from the skies of southern England. Hitler approved.

So, even while operations were continuing against the French, the Germans began to develop the captured airfields of northern France, Belgium, Holland, and Norway so that they could support most of the strength of the *Luftwaffe*. Streams of supplies and equipment came to these fields by road and railroad, to build up enough reserve

33

Junkers JU-87 dive bomber

stocks to undertake a sustained offensive effort by thousands of airplanes.

After the defeat of France, Hitler ordered his staffs to prepare a plan for the invasion of England. This plan was given the code name of Operation SEA LION. At the same time he ordered Goering to start probing the British air defenses, and to attack ports and shipping along the south coast of England. These preliminary operations began on July 10.

Then, on July 19, before he had set a definite date for the cross-Channel invasion, Hitler made a peace offer to the British. When this was contemptuously refused by Churchill, Hitler ordered Goering to prepare for an immediate full-scale aerial assault.

Fighter Command — and Radar

THE TWO PRINCIPAL COMPONENTS of the Royal Air Force were its Bomber Command — with the mission of undertaking offensive

British Hurricane fighter plane.

bombing attacks against the enemy — and its Fighter Command. Responsibility for the air defense of Great Britain rested on the shoulders of the commander of Fighter Command — Air Chief Marshal Dowding. As we have seen, he had felt that he needed at least 900 serviceable fighter planes to meet the kind of attack he expected the Germans would be able to make against England. On June 22, after the last Royal Air Force planes had returned from France, he had only slightly more than 550 planes. About two thirds of these were Hurricanes; the remainder were Spitfires, plus a very few older models, not so good as either Hurricanes or Spitfires. To back up the fighter planes there were about 3,500 antiaircraft guns — this was 2,000 less than were needed to protect England's cities and vital military installations.

But Fighter Command had two advantages about which the Germans knew nothing. One of these was a command and control system that permitted Dowding and his four group commanders to send their planes directly to the spots where they were needed. At Fighter

British Blenheim IV. This medium-range bomber was used also as a night fighter.

German fighter plane, the Focke-Wulf 190.

*British Spitfire fighter plane,
Mark XI.*

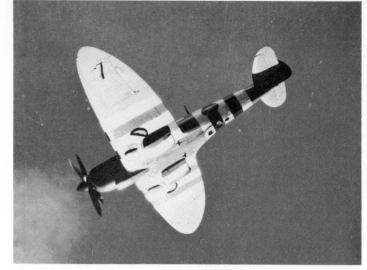

Junkers dive bomber, JU-88.

The Luftwaffe's *Heinkel bomber,
HE-111.*

HOW FIGHTER COMMAND WORKED

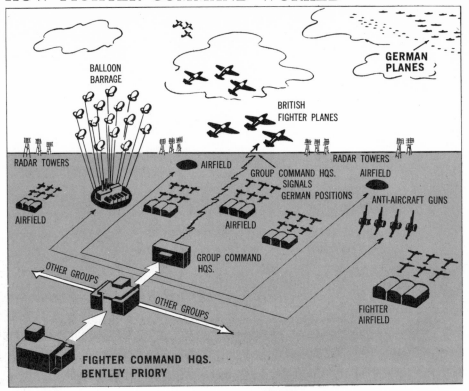

BALLOON BARRAGE

GERMAN PLANES

BRITISH FIGHTER PLANES

RADAR TOWERS

AIRFIELD

GROUP COMMAND HQS. SIGNALS GERMAN POSITIONS

RADAR TOWERS

AIRFIELD

ANTI-AIRCRAFT GUNS

AIRFIELD

AIRFIELD

OTHER GROUPS

GROUP COMMAND HQS.

OTHER GROUPS

FIGHTER AIRFIELD

FIGHTER COMMAND HQS. BENTLEY PRIORY

Command Headquarters, and at each of the group headquarters, the underground command posts contained gigantic maps on which the locations of all friendly and enemy air units could be plotted. By means of radio reports, these positions could be kept accurately located all of the time. Control officers kept a constant watch on these maps, and sent radio orders to the nearest Fighter Command units, on the ground or in the air, to meet each threat. No other country in the world had such a highly developed system of ground control for fighter defense.

The key element of this control system was the other surprise for the Germans. This was radar.

During the 1930's, electronic scientists of England, Germany, and America had all discovered the principle of radar. This was to send out powerful, high-frequency radio impulses which would be bounced back off of any large object in the sky. These radio "echoes" would then be reflected on a large cathode tube, which looked very much like a television screen. By means of the position of these echoes on the screens, radar operators could tell the location, height, and direction of any airplanes within the range of the radar impulses.

The British made somewhat more progress with this invention than did either the Germans or Americans, and they immediately put their knowledge to use. In 1937 the first radar station in the world was turned over to the Royal Air Force. That same year, the Royal Air Force began to construct a series of stations along the shores of England, and by the end of 1938, they were already able to track most planes arriving from the North Sea or English Channel. By June of 1940 there were fifty-one radar stations, covering most of the coast of England, particularly on the south and east, where enemy air raids would be most likely to strike. Regardless of clouds, day or night, these stations could pick up any incoming planes at distances

A single British Hurricane engages twelve Messerschmitt fighting planes in battle.

HALF ROLLS OFF THE TOP OF HIS LOOP

DESTROYS ANOTHER & DAMAGES A THIRD

BREAKS OFF, UNDAMAGED

SWOOPS UPWARDS & SHOOTS DOWN REAR AIRCRAFT

SINGLE HURRICANE MEETS 12 MESSERSCHMITTS HEAD-ON

DIVES UNDER THEM

A Heinkel bombing plane, HE-111, attacks London by daylight.

of 50 to 120 miles. As soon as a "blip" appeared on one of these radar screens, it was immediately reported to the operations headquarters, where the ground control system took over.

The Germans had suspected that the British were working with radar, and had sent Zeppelins and other aircraft along the coast of England to try to detect the radar impulses. But they listened on the wrong frequencies, so they failed to pick up anything. For this reason they believed that the English did not have an operating radar system. They soon learned differently.

40

The Preliminary Phase, July 10—August 12

DURING THE PERIOD before Hitler gave his final orders for Operation SEA LION, Goering completed his arrangements for the air assault. He assigned three air fleets to the task of destroying the Royal Air Force's Fighter Command. Air Fleet Two, under Field Marshal Kesselring, was based in Holland and Belgium; Air Fleet Three, commanded by Field Marshal Sperrle, was in northern France; and Air Fleet Five, under General Hans-Juergen Stumpff, was located in Norway. Stumpff's force was much smaller than the other two, and consisted only of long-range bombers and a few twin-engined Messerschmitt 110 long-range fighters. The total strength of the three air fleets was about 2,800 combat planes, with an operational strength of some 950 fighters and 1,300 bombers. Several hundred replacement planes of all types were ready to replace losses.

Beginning July 10 the Germans began to probe the fighter defenses of Britain by making attacks on seaports and on coastal ship-

Bombing formation of HE-111's on its way to Britain.

ping off southern and eastern England. From this they expected to learn something about the location, organization, and tactics of the British defenders. By the end of July they had learned enough to realize that radar was being used against them, and so they expanded their attacks to hit radar stations. They also attacked fighter airfields near the coast.

During the last two weeks of June, and early in July, Air Chief Marshal Dowding had been able to build up his force to 52 squadrons, totaling over 850 airplanes. But only about 650 of these were operational, or ready to fight; the others were being repaired, or undergoing maintenance, or otherwise unable to take part in the fighting. So Dowding still considered that he was about 250 planes short of what he required. He had 270 planes in reserve, but these

Antiaircraft batteries in Hyde Park, London.

*German planes bomb
Portland Harbor, in
the south of England.*

were needed for replacements; he had no trained pilots for them, anyway. It was the shortage of pilots that worried him most, and that would continue to worry him throughout the battle.

As the Germans opened their preliminary, probing attacks, they tried to entice the Royal Air Force into battle in order to find out the locations of English airfields and to reduce Fighter Command's operational strength before the main air assault. The British soon realized the German intentions, so they fought only hard enough to discourage the Germans from penetrating inland, and saved their strength for the larger attacks, which they expected would come soon.

On August 5, Hitler issued the orders for Operation SEA LION. The cross-Channel invasion was scheduled to take place during the first two weeks of September. Goering was ordered to start the aerial assaults to gain command of the air. Goering issued orders to his *Luftwaffe.* "Eagle Day" — the day set for the start of the *Luftwaffe's* full-scale effort — was to be August 13.

London aflame following a Nazi air attack.

The Battle of Britain—the Crisis

First German Assault Phase, August 13-23

ON "EAGLE DAY" the *Luftwaffe* flew 1,485 sorties, or combat missions, against England. There was heavy fighting in the air over the Channel and the south English coast. Some German planes even penetrated into central England. The British shot down 45 of the attacking planes, and lost 13 of their own. But German pressure mounted.

On August 15, the Germans flew 1,786 sorties — the largest number of planes they sent out on any day of the battle. Five major battles were fought over an area which extended in a 500-mile arc from southwest to northeast England. After a long day of furious combat, the Germans had lost 75 planes, the British 34. The Germans, however, announced that they had shot down 134 British planes while losing only 34 of their own, while the British claimed they had destroyed 182 German planes.

These claims were typical of those that would be announced by both sides throughout the battle. British claims were calculated from reports of the pilots and of ground observers, and they were usually about twice as high as the actual German losses. It was impossible to make an accurate count of wrecked German planes. Many of them were shot down over the sea, and some that appeared to go down in flames actually reached the French coast. The figures could never be checked accurately until *Luftwaffe* records were captured after the war. The Germans, on the other hand, deliberately gave out incorrect figures for propaganda reasons and to keep their own pilots from becoming discouraged. The Germans usually claimed about five times as many victims as they actually shot down, while admitting only about half of their own losses.

A Dornier bombing plane, DO-17, fights it out with a British Spitfire.

And so, with false or incorrect claims on both sides, the air battle over Britain continued to rage. Now, in addition to attacking British seaports and fighter bases, the Germans struck at radar installations and aircraft plants. But they were never able to knock out any complete section of the radar chain. No matter how much damage they inflicted, the installations were usually functioning again in a day or so. The results of German attacks on aircraft factories were equally ineffective in the long run. German planes destroyed many small plants, yet, during August, the British produced 476 Hurricanes and Spitfires — only twenty less than in July.

The German Junkers 87 (Stuka) dive bombers were taking the

The citizens of Yarmouth, England, battle the flames that followed a German bombing raid in April, 1941.

heaviest losses. They were slower than the Dorniers and other high-level bombers, and so they needed more fighter protection. The Royal Air Force pilots had discovered that if some of them engaged the German fighter cover in combat above the dive bombers, then other Hurricanes and Spitfires, guided in by ground control, could sweep in at lower levels to shoot down numbers of the Stukas. Goering did not have enough fighters to protect the dive bombers properly and so, on August 18, he ordered them out of the fight. This reduced his total attacking bomber force by almost one quarter.

The Second Assault Phase, August 24 – September 6

SINCE GERMAN LOSSES still continued to be heavy among the high-level bombers and fighters, Goering decided to concentrate the full efforts of all of his air fleets against the main inland Royal Air Force bases. He rightly believed that this would be the best way to reduce German losses, and at the same time to cripple the British Fighter Command.

The assaulting forces were massed together in larger groups of bombers, each group protected by at least one hundred of the formidable Messerschmitt fighters. By sheer weight of numbers the Germans consistently broke through to the Royal Air Force airfields and to Fighter Command's communications and control centers. German losses were heavy, but German planes were inflicting severe damage upon the defenders in the air and on the ground. They put some British airfields out of action for one or two days at a time, immobilizing many of the Royal Air Force planes, and destroying large numbers on the ground in follow-up raids.

By September 5 there was grave concern in the top command of British Fighter Command and in the British government. Reserve stocks of planes had fallen below two hundred; losses of irreplaceable pilots were rising. The remaining pilots, forced to go out day after day to meet enemy attacks, were close to exhaustion. Ground control was in grave difficulty due to the losses of radio stations, telephone lines, and cables. Churchill later reported the situation in these words:

"In the fighting between August 24 and September 6, the scales had tilted against Fighter Command. During these crucial days the Germans had continuously applied powerful forces against the airfields of South and Southeast England. . . . There was anxiety at Fighter Headquarters at Stanmore, and particularly at the headquarters of Number Eleven Fighter Group at Uxbridge. Extensive damage had been done to five of the group's forward airfields. . . . If the enemy had persisted . . . the whole intricate organization of Fighter Command might have broken down."

A German photograph of the damage that resulted from an air attack on the Royal Air Force field at Lympne, a fifteenth-century town in Kent, England.

The Germans did not realize how badly they had hurt Fighter Command. All they knew was that they were still taking heavy punishment from the Royal Air Force Spitfires and Hurricanes, and that these seemed to be always concentrated against German attacks, no matter how the *Luftwaffe* changed its tactics. Then, on September 6, while Goering was still puzzling out how to handle the situation, the Royal Air Force's Bomber Command carried out a long-range raid against Berlin.

The Attacks on London, September 7-30

At the very beginning of World War II, Goering had promised the German people that the Allies would never be able to strike the German capital. For that reason, as much as any other, he was infuriated by the British raid on Berlin. Hitler was equally enraged. The two Nazi chieftains immediately decided that London should be made to suffer. They both believed that terror attacks against the British capital, by day and night, would not only weaken the morale of the British people, but would also force the Royal Air Force to fight so desperately and so recklessly in defense of London that they would take heavy losses.

Despite the objections of some of the leading German airmen, Goering suddenly called off the *Luftwaffe* assaults against Fighter Command airfields and control installations, and Hitler ordered the *Luftwaffe* to begin a massive and intensive attack against the city of London. At the same time, Goering increased the number of fighters escorting each group of German bombers. He was sure he could destroy Fighter Command in the air, even though he had failed to knock it out on the ground.

Goering and Hitler could not have made a more foolish mistake. If Goering had continued his attacks against Fighter Command, his

A British civilian starts out for his post to watch for German parachutists.

A barrage balloon floats over defense works and emergency water pipes next to the British House of Parliament.

Luftwaffe might have won the battle and the war for Germany.

As it turned out, the German air attacks on London just made the British people more angry at the Nazis and more determined to win the war. Fighter Command, moreover, was now able to concentrate its efforts in one area, and so it began to take an increasingly heavy toll of the attackers.

Meanwhile, Hitler had been waiting to set the exact date for Operation SEA LION. It was obvious to him that Fighter Command had not been eliminated, but Goering insisted that the British were about to crack. He assured Hitler that he was now luring them into a last desperate and hopeless fight to save London. Hitler, therefore, awaited a final decision, tentatively setting September 27 as the day for the invasion.

During the night of September 13-14, the Royal Air Force's Bomber Command and small surface ships of the Royal Navy made a joint attack against the ports of France and the Low Countries where the Germans were assembling barges and ships for the planned invasion. The bombs and naval shellfire destroyed almost two hundred barges

— one tenth of the total the Germans had collected for their invasion of Britain. Next day, at a staff meeting, Grand Admiral Erich Raeder said to Hitler: "The present air situation does not provide the conditions for carrying out the operation because the risk is still too great." But Goering demanded one more chance, and Hitler agreed.

On September 15 the *Luftwaffe* sent over more than one thousand bombers and nearly seven hundred fighters in their greatest daylight attack on London. From noon to dusk, wave after wave of German planes came over the Channel and into the London area. Fighter Command was ready and waiting. Few of the German planes reached the center of the city. By the end of the day the *Luftwaffe* had lost fifty-six planes; Fighter Command had lost only twenty-six.

German invasion barges concentrated in the harbor at Boulogne, France.

On September 17, Hitler canceled the proposed invasion of September 27. The Germans now realized that they had lost the air battle, but they did not want to advertise the fact by breaking it off too quickly. They made a few more small daylight raids, and one last large one on September 30. That day Fighter Command shot down forty-seven German planes, and lost only twenty.

Final Phase, October 1-31

THE GERMANS now withdrew their bombers from daylight operations over Britain in order to get them ready for the heavier night raids that they planned to continue through the winter. Only a semblance of daylight aerial activity continued, with German fighter-bombers (fighter planes carrying bombs) making a number of hit-and-run raids over southern England. They inflicted relatively little damage, and they rarely stayed to fight the Royal Air Force defenders.

On October 12 Hitler postponed Operation SEA LION indefinitely. All of the invasion barges disappeared from the ports opposite southern England. During the next two weeks the German daytime raids dwindled steadily.

By the end of the month the Battle of Britain had come to an end. From July 10 to October 31, the Royal Air Force had shot down 1,733 German planes. It had lost 915 of its own planes in combat.

Had Goering and his *Luftwaffe* been successful, Germany would most certainly have invaded and conquered England, and World War II would have ended before either Russia or the United States were involved. World history would have been completely altered. This is why most historians and most military men consider the Battle of Britain to have been one of the most decisive conflicts ever fought. It was certainly the most decisive battle of World War II.

PLANE LOSSES

IN THE BATTLE OF BRITAIN JULY 10-OCTOBER 31, 1940

GERMAN PLANES LOST

1,733

BRITISH PLANES LOST

915

The superior maneuverability and firepower of the Spitfires and Hurricanes had overcome the more numerous and faster German fighter planes. They were able to do this, and at the same time take a heavy toll of the well-armed German bombers, largely because of the excellent Royal Air Force ground control system — and particularly because of radar.

To carry on this fight day after day, against tremendous odds, for almost four months, the pilots of Fighter Command had to have magnificent leadership, superb skill, and, above all, the courage and determination for which the British are so renowned. As Winston Churchill said, in reporting the results of the battle to the British people, "Never in the field of human conflict was so much owed by so many to so few."

The "Blitz" Over London and Malta

"London Can Take It"

DURING THE MONTH OF OCTOBER, 1940, the Germans had made fewer and fewer daylight assaults against Britain, but they began to step up their night bombing attacks on London and other large British cities. The Battle of Britain had proven to Hitler and Goering that they could not defeat the Royal Air Force's Fighter Command, but they still believed that they could break the spirit of the British people by terror bombardments.

Night after night the German planes came over the North Sea and the English Channel to drop their explosive and incendiary bombs on the crowded cities of Britain. The British radars could see them coming, and the Royal Air Force ground control system could send fighter planes to try to intercept them, but the pilots of the single-seater Spitfires and Hurricanes could rarely find the German planes in the dark skies. To make it more difficult, the Germans frequently staged their raids on cloudy and stormy nights.

In the darkness, of course, the Germans had difficulties, too. They could not see the blacked-out English cities very well and so, in order to locate their targets, they had to rely on directional radio beams from France and Germany. Whether the sky was clear or cloudy, these beacons could send the planes toward their targets and tell them where to drop their bombs. The system was not very accurate, but the Germans knew that bombs dropped anywhere near the center of a large city like London would cause great damage.

The British had a few night fighter planes. These were twin-seater fighters, fitted with radar sets and manned by a pilot, and a copilot, who was a radar operator. But the radars on these planes

Protective pattern of flak and tracer bullets over London.

British Beaufighter plane, carrying improved radar equipment in its nose.

could get the English pilots only to within a hundred yards of the attacking planes. Then the pilot and the copilot had to strain their eyes to try to see an exhaust flame, or the flicker of an instrument light, on one of the German bombers. Sometimes they were successful, and were able to shoot down one of the invaders. But usually the Germans reached their targets and dropped their bombs without interference.

Almost every night hundreds of English men, women, and children were killed and injured, while thousands more were made homeless by the destruction of their houses. The British government did not know whether their people could stand this much longer or not. Yet as the ordeal continued, week after week, month after month, Churchill discovered that his fellow countrymen remained as firm as he in their determination to outlast the Nazis.

Every night hundreds of thousands of people trooped into emergency air-raid shelters, laughing and joking about sleeping together in crowded quarters. In London large sections of the "tube," or subway system, had been converted into underground shelters.

Warehouses and barges on the Thames set afire by German raiders.

Destruction in Coventry, England, following an all-night attack by German planes.

At the same time, many thousands of men and women, organized into fire watcher teams, waited bravely on rooftops throughout the night, while bombs hurtled down beside them. The task of these people was to try to put out any German incendiary bombs that fell on roofs, and to help the efficient National Fire Service keep the many fires from raging out of control. And every day, despite frequent deadly explosions, hundreds of the most courageous English men and women expertly extracted the fuses from German delayed-action bombs.

One of the worst raids of the war hit the city of Coventry on the night of November 14-15, 1940. Almost five hundred German bombers were in the attacking force. Hundreds of people were killed and thousands injured. The famous Coventry Cathedral was demolished, as was most of the center of the city. The Germans hoped that attacks like these would keep people from going to work. However, the aircraft factories in Coventry continued to turn out planes without interruption.

THE "BLITZ" DESTROYED OR DAMAGED

ONE   OUT OF FIVE BRITISH HOMES

Soldiers from British convalescent hospitals attend service in bombed Coventry Cathedral.

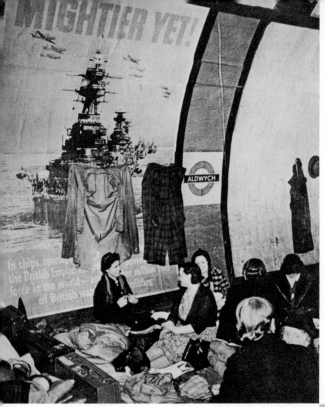

Civilians take refuge in a London subway during an air raid.

The Church of Saint Mary Le Bow in London after a night raid by German bombers.

Another great raid hit London on the evening of December 29. Huge sections of the city were wiped out by explosions and fires. But instead of frightening the Londoners, this simply made them angry. They cheered Churchill when he visited their ruined homes, and they asked him to send British bombers to strike back against Germany. Churchill decided that "London can take it."

British scientists had already developed a number of protective measures to save lives and to reduce property damage. Now they were trying to find ways to keep the Germans from hitting their targets. Very early during the "blitz" British scientists had discovered that they could distort the German radio beacons that guided the *Luftwaffe* pilots to their targets. Soon more than half of the German bombs were falling miles away from where they were supposed to fall. Most fell in open fields or in the sea, where they did little damage. Every time the Germans tried a new radio directional system, the British scientists found a way to ruin it.

The British were also developing new and effective antiaircraft rockets. They installed these in great numbers in and around London, and by spring of 1941, the rockets were beginning to take a heavy toll of the attacking planes. Seventy raiding bombers were shot down by these rockets in the first two weeks of May, 1941. These losses, added to the demands of other operations in Europe and the Mediterranean, were too much for Goering. He gave up the attacks on Britain.

Again the *Luftwaffe* had failed in a major effort to knock Britain out of the war. England had suffered severely. Between June, 1940, when the Battle of Britain began, and May, 1941, when the "blitz" over London ended, more than 43,000 civilians had been killed, and another 51,000 seriously injured. The British people, however, were more confident than ever that they would eventually win the war.

The Early Air War in North Africa and the Mediterranean

ITALY ENTERED THE WAR in June, 1940, just before the surrender of France. The entire Italian air strength of about fifteen hundred combat aircraft was available for operations against the British in the Mediterranean, North Africa, and East Africa — the area the British called the Middle East. At this time the Royal Air Force had about four hundred combat planes in the Middle East, and many of these were older and slower than the Italian planes. Most of the British planes were in Egypt, but some were stationed at Malta, and others were in East Africa.

In the fall of 1940, Italian Field Marshal Rodolfo Graziani invaded northwestern Egypt from Libya. His army was supported by about five hundred combat aircraft. Soon after this, another Italian

A Royal Air Force formation of Boston bombers rises from a desert airfield in clouds of dust.

Italian Breda assault aircraft, BA-65.

army invaded Greece from Albania. General Sir Archibald Wavell, commanding British forces in the Middle East, sent a few Royal Air Force units to help the Greeks stop the Italian invasion of their country, and this left him only about two hundred planes to support his main army in Egypt.

In December, 1940, even though his forces were greatly outnumbered on the ground and in the air, General Wavell directed an amazing counterattack against the Italians in Egypt. The British planes soon swept the Italians from the skies over Egypt and Libya, then helped Wavell's troops in smashing Graziani's army. In later operations in early 1941, the Royal Air Force gave the same kind of close support to the British forces that conquered Italian colonies in East Africa.

Hitler decided to send reinforcements to help the Italians in North Africa, and placed General Erwin Rommel in command of the Axis forces in Libya. But Hitler and Rommel soon discovered that British air and naval units based on Malta were taking a heavy toll of the transports carrying supplies and reinforcements to Rommel's German and Italian troops.

The Royal Air Force makes a direct hit on a German airfield in the desert.

The Battle of Malta

ITALIAN AIRPLANES based in Sicily and south Italy had been attacking Malta for several months, but they had been unable to stop the British air and naval raids against Axis convoys. For this reason, in January, 1941, Hitler transferred the Tenth German Air Fleet from Norway to Sicily. The *Luftwaffe* soon established air superiority over the central Mediterranean and began a series of heavy bombardments of Malta. German planes sank a British aircraft carrier and a cruiser convoying supplies to Malta, and they damaged a number of other British vessels.

The British realized how important Malta was to them, however, and continued to reinforce the island with planes and ships. For almost a year a seesaw air and sea battle took place around the tiny island, with the British inflicting almost as much damage as they received.

In December, 1941, Hitler sent *Luftwaffe* Field Marshal Kesselring to take command of all Axis forces in Italy and Sicily. Kesselring was given an additional German air fleet — the Second — with which to gain complete control of the air over the central Mediterranean. From then on, German and Italian air raids against Malta increased

A British Mosquito fighter plane flies out of Malta.

in both number and intensity. By March, 1942, the *Luftwaffe* was hitting Malta with as many as a hundred planes ten times a day.

These attacks soon destroyed all the Royal Air Force planes on the island, and forced the remaining British warships based on Malta to move away. In May, 1942, Kesselring reported to Hitler that Malta was completely neutralized.

Despite the German air attacks, however, the Royal Navy continued to send supplies to the battered little island, protecting each supply ship with several destroyers, cruisers, and battleships. More Spitfires were flown in from British and American carriers. Increasing numbers of Royal Air Force fighters and planes of longer range began to challenge German control of the air over Malta. By September, 1942, they were actually raiding German bases in Italy and Sicily. Kesselring still held the advantage in total numbers of planes available, but he could no longer claim complete air superiority over the Mediterranean.

Operations in the Balkans and Crete

German Invasion of the Balkans

SOON AFTER the beginning of the air Battle of Malta, the *Luftwaffe* moved into southeastern Europe in support of German attacks on Yugoslavia and Greece. Before dawn on April 6, 1941, more than one thousand planes of the Fourth German Air Fleet struck Yugoslavian airfields from bases in Romania and Hungary. The tiny Yugoslavian air force was quickly wiped out.

The *Luftwaffe* then shifted to strike Belgrade, the capital of Yugoslavia, in an intensive three-day assault. By the time this attack

German Stuka dive bombers in Greece.

was over, more than seventeen thousand Yugoslav civilians lay dead in the rubble of the shattered city. The government and the central military headquarters were cut off from the Yugoslav field armies, which were now being smashed by invading columns of German tanks and infantry. It was the same story as in the previous German campaigns. The cold-blooded efficiency of the *Luftwaffe* and the *Wehrmacht* quickly overcame all opposition. The Yugoslav army surrendered on April 17.

Things were only slightly different in Greece. General Wavell had sent additional air and ground units to help the Greeks, and these put up a much more effective resistance for several days. But combined German and Italian ground attacks soon drove the Greek army back, and the English were also forced to withdraw. Then the *Luftwaffe* planes that had overwhelmed Yugoslavia joined the battle in Greece. The outnumbered Royal Air Force pilots were soon driven out of the skies. The few surviving British planes were withdrawn to Crete and Egypt. The British army was forced to fight its way to the beaches, where it was evacuated by the Royal Navy, with some air cover provided by carrier planes of the Mediterranean Fleet Air Arm. Greece surrendered on April 23.

Battle of Crete

THE GERMANS now made immediate plans to seize Crete. Because the Royal Navy still controlled the waters of the Mediterranean, Hitler and his staff decided that the operation should be carried out by the *Luftwaffe*. Goering was directed to conquer Crete by combined aerial bombardment and airborne attack.

Luftwaffe General Alexander Loehr was in immediate command of the operation. He had available 650 combat aircraft, 650 troop-

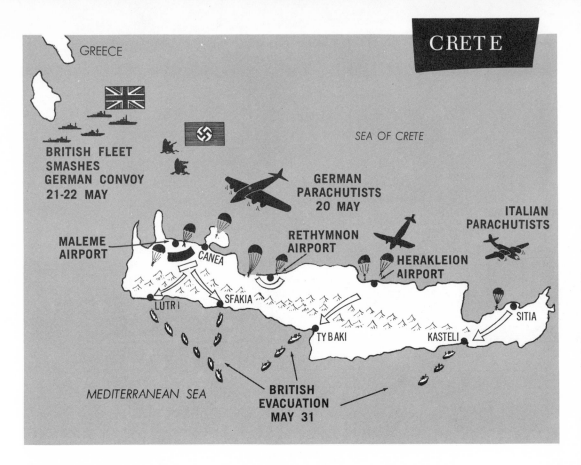

GREECE

BRITISH FLEET
SMASHES
GERMAN CONVOY
21-22 MAY

SEA OF CRETE

GERMAN
PARACHUTISTS
20 MAY

ITALIAN
PARACHUTISTS

MALEME
AIRPORT

CANEA

RETHYMNON
AIRPORT

HERAKLEION
AIRPORT

SFAKIA

LUTRI

SITIA

TYBAKI

KASTELI

MEDITERRANEAN SEA

BRITISH
EVACUATION
MAY 31

CRETE

carrying transport planes, and 100 gliders, plus two army divisions. The initial airborne assault was to be made by the 7th Parachute Division; the 5th Mountain Division would later be flown in to airfields captured by the paratroopers.

The preliminary German aerial bombardment of Crete began in early May. Every day fleets of two hundred to three hundred planes struck at the three British airfields at Maleme, Rethymnon, and Heraklion. These attacks soon drove the few Royal Air Force survivors back to Egypt. At the same time, German planes struck relentlessly against British warships, forcing the Royal Navy to stay away from the waters around Crete during daylight hours.

71

A German troop carrier is shot down over Crete.

Early on May 20, the German bombers carried out one final, intensive assault against the British army units defending the three airfields. Suddenly parachutes bloomed in the air over Maleme. Despite their losses under the bombardment, the British were ready, and a terrific ground battle soon was raging all around the airfield. *Luftwaffe* fighter planes gave close support to the airborne invaders. Later in the day, more German paratroopers dropped from the sky, this time over Rethymnon and Heraklion. The struggles that took place were as fierce as at Maleme.

Meanwhile, some of the German soldiers at Maleme had captured part of the airfield. *Luftwaffe* transport planes immediately began to land, and out jumped more German soldiers to join the fight. Most of these planes were wrecked in bomb craters on the field, and others were destroyed by British artillery, but a few got away to return to Greek airfields. There they picked up more German

72

A German plane crashes on the island of Crete.

soldiers and flew them back to Crete.

Few conflicts in history have been as hard-fought, or as closely contested, as was the Battle of Crete. The bravery of soldiers on both sides was outstanding. But it was the efficiency and courage of the *Luftwaffe* pilots that finally swung the battle in the Germans' favor. German light bombers and fighter planes gave close support to the embattled paratroopers, who had no artillery to reply to the British guns. At the same time other *Luftwaffe* fighter planes and dive bombers kept any Royal Air Force or Royal Navy units from entering the fight. And the whole time, at all three airfields, the German transport pilots brought their planes in with more reinforcements, despite British antiaircraft guns and a hail of direct fire from British cannon, machine guns, and rifles.

German losses were terrible in the early days of the battle. Several companies and battalions of paratroopers were practically wiped out. One quarter of the transport planes were destroyed, and many more damaged. But as more planes and more German soldiers arrived on the embattled airfields, they were finally able to push the British out of range. Then the fields were repaired, and the remaining transport planes brought in their loads of reinforcements and supplies with fewer losses. By May 26, all three German positions were secure, and the Germans had gained a clear advantage over the exhausted British, who could no longer protect themselves from ceaseless aerial bombardment and strafing.

Once more the Royal Navy moved in to evacuate British army troops from a *blitzkrieg* defeat. This time there was no air support, either from the Royal Air Force or from the Fleet Air Arm; the last British carrier in the Mediterranean had been knocked out of action by German bombers. British army and navy casualties were heavy, and several warships were sunk in a never-ceasing battle between the *Luftwaffe* and the British Mediterranean Fleet. The Royal Navy managed to evacuate about half of the thirty thousand British troops on Crete; the remainder were killed or captured by the Germans. The Royal Navy lost four cruisers and six destroyers in the Battle of Crete. One carrier, three battleships, and several more cruisers and destroyers were badly damaged.

The *Luftwaffe* had won its greatest victory.

Index